THE ENTREPRENEUR'S FIELD GUIDE: How to Thrive in the Unknown

NICHOLAS CROWN

Copyright © 2023 Nicholas Crown

All rights reserved. No part of this book may be reproduced or transmitted in any form or by any means, electronic or mechanical, including photocopying, recording, or by any information storage and retrieval system, without permission in writing from the author.

Cover design by **Numeral Studio**

Published by **Harrington Books**

ISBN: 979-8-218-22868-2

Printed in the United States

Only when you're comfortable not knowing
will you find your way.

13	**INTRO**: Letter to an Explorer	
17	**PREFACE**: Why a Field Guide?	

19	**Section 1:** **THE LIMITLESS** **UNKNOWN**	Enter the Woods My Map Isn't Your Map—and That's Okay It Ain't Like the Movies

31	**Section 2:** **TAKING INVENTORY**	Who Are You? Who Aren't You? Environmental Imprinting Futurecasting Embrace the Now

45	**Section 3:** **MAKING YOUR** **FIRST STEP**	The Power of Iteration Running Micro-Tests Learning and Review

53	**Section 4:** **ENCOUNTERING** **OTHER EXPLORERS**	The Guardian of the Status Quo The False Guide The Thief The Elder The Humble Traveler

61	**Section 5:** **GENERAL HAZARDS** **AND ANTIDOTES**	Uninformed Investing Thinking You Know Thinking Someone Else Knows Hard Work Is a Lie The Startup Martyr
81	**Section 6:** **BREAKING GROUND**	From a Seed: Building 　Something New From Propagation: Buying 　Something Cheaply Grafting: Combining Experience
89	**Section 7:** **THE SEASONS**	The Season of Confusion The Season of Iteration The Season of Choice The Season of Risk
103	**Section 8:** **UNCOVERING HIDDEN** **TREASURE**	
109	**Section 9:** **HOMECOMING**	
115	**BONUS:** DISCOVERY WORKSHEET	

Letter to an Explorer

To the Explorer,
Iterate or die.

This is the tattoo inked on your arm before you enter the woods. It's *that* important not to forget. You can see my own shadowy tattoo underneath my dress shirts if you look closely enough.

Here, in the dense woods, things never stay the same. In fact, my personal map is useless to you—it's already obsolete. The path you're walking is only revealed with each hesitant step and becomes obscured the moment you turn around. You never quite know exactly where you are in this vast thicket. Some days the sun never shines. And the days of the week become meaningless.

In these woods, you're so lost that you can only approximate your proper bearings with intuition and a few crude tools and principles.

In here, you're never certain of anything.

A contemporary explorer is nowhere without his or her GPS. When that GPS battery fails and you're unaware of the deeper language of the wilderness, you're as good as dead in a few days. And when you die in the woods, nobody remembers you.

But you have a direction: Just roll up your sleeve, and look at the motto boldly inked onto your forearm.

What are these woods, exactly?

Some might call them the Kingdom of the Unknown, where many persist in a state of desperation, clawing for reality. This is the world outside the warm cocoon of your parents' home or a stable salary. Nothing's stranger than the desire to leave the known and enter the unknown—and nothing's more worthwhile.

I'll be direct: The quest for wealth and personal freedom in the woods, in the unknown, begins with creating something on your own. Or if you prefer a fancy word, let's call it *entrepreneurship*.

You may be considering this path from a quiet retreat in a thousand-dollar office chair overlooking the skyline or perhaps an overturned mop bucket in the break room of a convenience store. It doesn't really matter where you start. The rules are the same for the privileged and unprivileged alike.

This is far from another manual of tips sprinkled with charming anecdotes from some billionaire's life. No, this is a true field guide—the rules for survival—that will allow you to sidestep many of the blunders that cost me millions of dollars, friends, lovers, and years I'll never get back.

Unless you grew up in the Alaskan backwoods or some other rural pocket of our world, you may not yet know that there's a very funny thing about the woods. And that is, when you know how the woods *operate*, everything clicks into place.

You can cozy up to the unknown.

When you're in command of this environment, the sun shines through the trees, and ravenous animals recede into their burrows. You marvel at the dew on leaves sparkling like diamonds all around you. You don't mind being a little lost. In fact, you approach it like an old friend.

This *Field Guide* shows you how the woods work, so that you'll feel at home in their misty branches.

Soon enough, you'll never need a map again.

Nicholas Crown

Why a Field Guide?

Rather than a book or a course, a field guide is a multipurpose tool for a dangerous journey. It's not a map, because a map only works for a particular trail—think of this more as a guardrail. A field guide serves you on *all* trails, likely for the rest of your life's journeys. It never goes out of style. You'll never need to worry about using the wrong map.

A field guide works even when certainty is low or zero.

If anything, a map provides a false sense of security. If I handed you one, you would cling so tightly to it that when you saw the actual terrain you'd be lost. Maps are what you see littered across social media with clickbait titles like *How I Made $10M with Drop-shipping*.

In fact, we become *more lost* than not having seen these false maps to begin with, because we abandon our entrepreneurial intuition and unquestioningly adopt something that supposedly worked for someone else. But their roads are never going to be your road. In the wilderness, it's solely *your* intuition, second only to *your* preparation, that will not only get you rich but also save your life.

With a field guide, you become aware of perils before venturing away from home. Can you put a price on preparedness? You may come across a viper or a poisonous frog or *you may not*. But if you do, you know to steer clear of touching it. You know that you can eat *one* mushroom for survival but not *that* one. The red flags are presented in advance. Your mental load lightens, allowing you to focus on higher order tasks. Your journey may be long or short, but you must be prepared.

In the environment of entrepreneurship, or that of living a life of value and sharing it with others, I couldn't possibly hand you a map, but I *can* provide guideposts and basic training. I promise that this is the most valuable gift I can offer you.

You will find yourself rereading this guide to refresh your memory as you move forward. You may even be tempted to share the principles that stand out to you with friends and family interested in venturing into the woods on their own one day. After all, *everyone* has the ability to succeed on this journey with enough persistence.

I forged this guide not only relying on my own experiences growing several multimillion-dollar businesses but also after interviewing highly successful entrepreneurs and cataloging their commonalities and underlying principles. There are literally tens of thousands of hours of experience distilled within this guide: Individually, each story is nothing short of astonishing. Yet amazingly, I discovered that there's an identifiable rhythm, a certain range of common actions, that lead to success. And since I've heard so many "wild rides" to success, I'm no longer surprised but rather stand in awe of the vast similarities that this *Field Guide* will reveal.

A state of surprise is what I hope to remove from your own entrepreneurial journey.

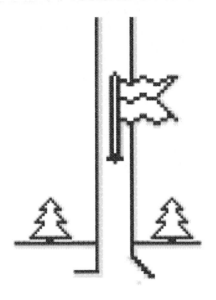

Section 1:

THE LIMITLESS UNKNOWN

As a child, I once wandered through the wooded area behind my house. Suddenly, the bend in the path I was tracking became obscured. Was the tall oak the marker for the way home? Or perhaps it was the gray boulder covered in moss? A red, plastic ribbon was nailed to a tree at my left suggesting danger in the near vicinity. My stomach sank.

I was lost.

The tall treetops swirled around me, and I felt as if they would swallow me whole. As I walked, occasionally tripping over branches and roots, I spotted a deer hunter in the distance. He recognized me as a child rather than his prey and, still squinting from behind his scope, shooed me away to a safer path. Tromping around, lost and directionless, I could have easily been shot.

Safely away from the hunter, I calculated I could probably take three or four different paths. One of them would have to return me to the backyard of my home.

Eventually, one of them did.

I didn't tell my parents what happened. Looking back, it seems that I defaulted to (1) relaxing and then (2) modeling my options, even as a child. Estimating the amount of time I had been walking, I eyeballed a few paths. My first guess had been toward the hunter. That was a dead end. My second guess was to follow the most well-worn path I could see.

This was my first memory of dealing with the pure unknown.

This state of confusion—and more importantly *guessing*—is familiar to entrepreneurs of all shapes and sizes. Their comfort with this "place" of not knowing is what helps them succeed far more than the other commonly described attributes, like grit, determination, and raw intelligence.

In fact, even in my more mature businesses today, I'm still guessing. When you hit a dead end (oftentimes far less risky than encountering the hunter that I did as a child), you simply try the next best path.

I've developed comfort with not knowing, and you will too.

Enter the Woods

There's very little that separates a hike in the woods from engaging in a new business venture. In fact, it's difficult to decipher where a hike ends and the business begins.

Because anything and everything can *become* a business, there's probably no other field of study as undefined as business.

Science becomes business the moment a drug goes to market. Singing in the shower becomes business if you go viral and sell merch. Even religion is a heck of a business. Can you go through life *without* transacting?

Maybe we should just call business "life" instead?

A business or entrepreneurial venture is:
- → Anything that generates value and returns a portion of that value back to the owner
- → Anything that may generate value in the future and potentially return a portion of that value back to the owner

The business that you've been taught in school isn't business at all. Memorizing random tidbits of accounting, finance, and marketing doesn't produce a businessperson any more than memorizing *Romeo and Juliet* transforms you into a romantic. The truth is that studying things narrowly, as if under a microscope, often has a deleterious effect.

Here is another way to look at business and opportunity:
- → When something existing can be produced faster or cheaper
- → When something entirely new is created that people want or need
- → When you see something that others cannot
- → When you can help others achieve something they couldn't before

Perhaps you hate the notion of business right off the bat. If all you know about business is from college, *The Wall Street Journal*, and clips of shareholder meetings,

I don't blame you.

Business is far more vibrant than that. In fact, it's an art form.

Business is the act of creating value in society. And this bears repeating, a business *must create value!* If your underwater basket-weaving skills aren't drawing a crowd of paying customers after ten years and dozens of oxygen tanks, you don't have a business—you have a hobby. Avoid getting the two confused.

When starting something new, by definition you have to *not know stuff* to get anything done. Because if you're creating something that nobody has done before, you have no template or any magic trick to see if it will work in advance.

> **Guidepost:** *A business can be many things, but it has to create value.*

To create original value, you have to enter the woods. And then you can only peer down at your tattoo and grit your teeth.

If life is impossible to define, so is business. Because business is the unknown.

Business *is* the woods.

My Map Isn't Your Map—and That's Okay

If I'm not you, how can I show you the way?

I am a sponge for information. I've taken advice from celebrities, athletes, academics—you name it—on how to run my life and businesses. In fact, I've pushed this to the limit by adopting obscure meditation, visualization, note-taking, and extreme diets I read about, all without a single consideration if it made sense for me in particular. These ill-fitting habits did nothing but slow me down, like a ludicrous five-minute golf warm-up sequence right before you slice the ball into a lake.

The longer I tried to enact *others'* ways of doing things, or *their* map, without success, the more frustrated I became. And what makes matters worse is you believe it's your fault for not engaging in the diet/exercise/ meditation intensely enough to get the desired results from the celebrity or influencer.

You're left feeling ashamed for failing. Meanwhile, the source of this false map gets away scot-free because— well, it worked for him.

How is this possible?

It comes down to this: When someone tells you *exactly* what to do or what *exactly* worked for them (if they remember, which they probably don't), they're handing over useless information.

> **Guidepost:** *Only you can sketch and refine your road map to getting what you want—no one else can do it for you.*

If I told you *exactly* what I did to get rich right now, it would be of absolutely no value to you.

You'll notice that I rarely reveal on social media specific strategies that worked for me and even then only for entertainment purposes. I know what I did won't work for you. That's why this is a field guide, not a you-can-do-what-I-did sales pitch.

If I shared a random sequence of steps, it would be meaningless to you and you wouldn't be able to follow it anyway.

Remember, you're absolutely nothing like me (consider yourself lucky). You have your own strengths and weaknesses that makes living on planet Earth an exciting, diverse experience. I wouldn't have it any other way.

Your map is unique in:
- → The time period in which you live
- → Your personal experience
- → The way you express your idea to the marketplace and others (your style)
- → Your interests and motivations

Telling you what I did doesn't empower you. In fact, it

hobbles you as you try to walk a road that doesn't exist. It's me giving you an impossible task masquerading as strategy and making money from it. It's actually evil because it steals your time—time you could be using to draft your own map!

The common phrase describing this situation is *showing you my winning Lotto number*. That's listing off the exact (read: random) combination of steps I took to achieve success. It technically shows you how I got rich (these Lotto numbers) but does little to help you get rich too.

Remember, I'm offering a *field guide,* not a map, preparing you for what you *might see* along the way. It doesn't tell you to take a right or a left at the bend. I'm not recommending to you a place to stay or to eat. Instead, it's a set of underlying principles to take with you along the way—*your* way.

Loosely sketch your own map by answering the following:
→ What is meaningful to you?
→ What would you create (not consume) for fun?
→ What can you do better than anyone else?
→ What opinion do you have that differs from most people?

Now, I could get philosophical, but my map simply can't be your map, because you're unique and wholly different from me. You wouldn't want to (or be capable) of replicating my map, so why bother?

That's why the frustration of replicating some

dropshipping (on-demand e-commerce fulfillment by a third party) or other flash-in-the-pan online schemes are losing prospects for those who try.

You can't do it exactly like the other guy, and you don't want to.

It Ain't Like the Movies

When I got to Wall Street, I couldn't believe how different it was from my imagination.

Nowhere to be found were the loudmouthed personalities from my favorite movies and books dropping sizzling one-liners. Rather, I was surrounded by disgruntled introverts fighting to make a buck. There was little comradery to be found. In fact, I made exactly *one* real friend in seven years in the business.

Even once I had begun to make more money years later, it was always lower in amount and far less satisfying to receive than I anticipated. Eventually, I left the business altogether. Looking back, it was the camaraderie and excitement that I was after far less than the money.

Today, I earn more money than ever compared to back when I was working for an investment bank, but most of my time is spent doing things I enjoy with amazing people.

I share this not to urge you to quit your job: That's for you to decide. However, you probably won't get rich the way you think you will. Let's look at another example.

A boxer needs to anticipate punches from his opponent. However, he doesn't know in exactly what order or the combination of punches his opponent will throw during the fight. He simply knows that punches will fly after he touches gloves with his opponent.

> **Guidepost:** *If you know it won't look exactly how you anticipated, you'll be less surprised when you see it.*

In comparison, reality makes even the bounded game of boxing look like child's play. Reality is too complex for our brains to get a hold of all at once because there aren't merely punches and jabs. The moves are limitless, and the rounds never end.

Be prepared for:
→ The first several paths to turn out to be dead ends
→ "Easy" problems ending up complex and costly
→ "Hard" problems ending up being easy to solve
→ Real life to never look like the Hollywood version of the thing you're chasing

General preparation far outweighs specific scenario-based anticipation. You're an entrepreneur, not a call-center operator with a fixed script.

So if you'll join me for a moment and open your mind wide, you'll eventually fill in the gaps with your own strategy in real time.

And it will be far better than any advice, map, or instructions that you could receive from anyone. Especially me.

The Limitless Unknown Summary

→ The sphere of building something is unknown
→ Wealth appears when you use your unique talent to deliver value to society
→ The path will look unfamiliar most of the time

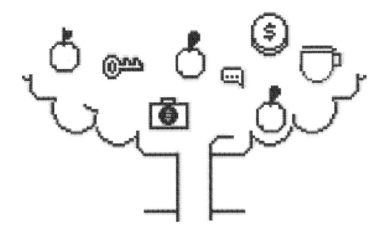

Section 2:

TAKING INVENTORY

As you exhale, try to see the unique nature of each tree from the denseness of the woods. Perhaps several are bearing fruit?

Isn't making money all about spotting opportunities such as this? That must be how the rich got there in the first place, right?

Yes and no.

Opportunity is a tricky word because it's commonly misunderstood as somewhere *out there*, rather than *in here*. Each opportunity is unique, each a result of your special disposition and experience rather than a hole in the market anyone could fill with a product or service. In other words, an opportunity that you cannot address isn't an opportunity to you—it's noise.

Let's think about it like this—if you saw that the LA Lakers were in need of, say, a better point guard, someone who could really facilitate stronger offense for the team and lead them to another championship, does it mean that you should step up for the job?

Even if you'd like to jump into the role of point guard because you've been shooting free throws in your backyard for years, you wouldn't be able to do it without a lifetime of professional basketball experience. Identifying an opportunity is useless unless you can specifically fill it.

> **Guidepost:** An opportunity is only real if you're the perfect individual to seize it—otherwise it's noise.

Alternatively, perceiving an opportunity that *anyone* could fill isn't an opportunity at all. This is the comical landscape of social media "business content." That's simply a game of musical chairs. Any scheme or opportunity with no barriers to entry will be immediately filled—this is why selling on Amazon (the e-commerce marketplace) and dropshipping has plenty of players, but few make money as they compete directly against one another and drive profit to zero. Except for those who teach others about dropshipping!

Social media is filled to the brim with talking heads spouting information about *obvious* moneymaking opportunities. They're about as useful as telling you to stand in on point guard for the Lakers.

It would be better had you never heard about the opportunity in the first place as it's (1) wasted your time and (2) distracted you from your interests.

Don't worry about opportunity. Focus on your particular role in adding value—the qualities or skills that only you can provide.

Who Are You?

You have both a unique disposition that you were born with and a perspective shaped by your life experiences. If you were singularly special at birth, you're even further distinguished by your lived experience. Therefore, right out of the gate, you're valuable.

The trick is identifying your unique aspects and applying them to a world that's hungry for solutions.

You can engage in the discovery process by asking others how they'd describe you, digging through your past interests and passions (even the ones you've tossed aside), or taking a personality test.

This step is non-negotiable, as it will save you from attempting unfulfilling tasks and endeavors that rob you of precious time.

To find your unique viewpoint you may:
→ Revisit your childhood or early teen hobbies
→ Ask your closest friends what you'd be good at
→ Take a personality assessment
→ Actively visualize dream or ideal scenarios

I suggest keeping a notebook of your responses to these questions; their clarity will improve over time. Without knowing who you are and what you want, you will be hard-pressed to find a way forward in the woods.

Additionally, you may want to explore:

- → What combinations of traits and interests make you one of a kind? (e.g., the lion-taming ballet dancer)
- → In what way are you best able to communicate your ideas? (music, visual art, writing, speech, etc.)
- → Who do you admire in the real world and why? List their characteristics.

When you know who you are, you can narrow down the best paths forward with more accuracy. When you don't know who you are, every step is a blind gamble.

Who Aren't You?

In 2009, the bank I was working for acquired Lehman Brothers from bankruptcy, for pennies on the dollar. The shake-up was so extreme in my group that my managing director (translation: my boss) was demoted, and I was transferred under another manager I had never met.

After the switch-up, every morning when I arrived at 5:30 a.m., my new boss was already there. And he lived in New Jersey, more than an hour away from our office in Manhattan. That means he was waking up around four o'clock in the morning every single day. Or perhaps, as I estimated, he never slept.

Another intern stood in awe of his omnipresence on the desk. I was horrified. I drew a vector in time from myself, in my twenties, to him, in his late fifties. I wanted to be nowhere near this desk at this ungodly hour in my fifties, hanging out with a bunch of twenty-something punks. His day-to-day life was my worst nightmare.

After verbalizing this sentiment to an intern next to me, he asked, "Then why are you here?"

I didn't have a good answer.

Having a clear example of what you *don't want* is just as helpful as knowing what you do.

If you prefer waterfalls, by all means take a closer look. If caves are of interest, crouch down and shine your flashlight into the darkness. If neither are of interest, keep walking until something strikes your fancy.

Don't bother wasting your time with things that don't interest you.

> **Guidepost:** *Look at the "future you," be it a boss, parent, or movie character, and ask yourself, "Do I want to be him or her?"*

What is fundamentally wrong with American specialization culture is that we specialize without having enough time to play around, so many find themselves like me, miraculously, in a job they hate. It's an idea born out of the Industrial Revolution during which we were best educated to occupy a specific role in the assembly line.

Recently, we've improved upon that concept with the "liberal arts" education—that's *try a little of this, a little of that*. The American college or university is designed to be a place to experiment. But it's tragically nowhere near the environment of the "real world" outside the manicured quads and neo-Gothic (if you're lucky) architecture. It doesn't work.

Experimenting academically has no "teeth." If you fail a class, you don't go broke and get your cafeteria card cut off. Further, the classroom environment doesn't even remotely resemble the reality of practicing the trade in the field.

Only once you leave the utopia of the college campus do you realize how much you need to learn.

Explore who you want to be and who you don't, and listen to your own internal feedback as you do, as early as possible.

Environmental Imprinting

New York had a way of rubbing off on me.

In 2008, I wasn't doing anything original. I merely chose the highest-paid option from the cardboard cutout lives we were offered upon graduation. When I showed up for work every day, it looked a lot like yesterday.

I wasn't an A player either—I was just proficient enough, mostly because I didn't care. I obsessed over the most minute details to set myself apart—a Rolex model or the color of my tie, a presentation skill or trading secret that I milked to death.

In Japan, they'd refer to me as a *salaryman*. In America, a wage slave.

I clung to my job title and brand-name clothing like life support.

This model that New York offered me works for millions of people, and I hold nothing against them. It just didn't work for me.

This was the false comfort and security of a high-salary job. And for me, remaining in the humdrum "known," as opposed to venturing into the woods where I belonged, was eating away at my soul.

Nevertheless, two things became apparent to me as I slogged my way through my career as a trader:
→ Technology was going to replace me
→ I didn't like what I did, for any amount of money they could've handed me

In a sense, I already knew I was going to lose here. There was no path I could draw where everything was going to work out.

Of course, I didn't have a choice into which geographic culture I was born—certainly it could have been far worse. However, I had a choice if I was going to stay.

Comforted by salary, I—
- → Clung to titles and status
- → Delivered the bare minimum (because I cared little about what I did)
- → Risked little, had limited upside
- → Didn't know and didn't care to find out (preferred entertainment)

So what's more terrifying? Occupying an environment where you know (or think you know) what each day will look like until one day in the near future you find yourself without a job?

Or to wander into the woods where anything could happen?

I quit my job on Wall Street in 2014 and started over.

By 2016, when I arrived in Miami, I saw something completely new. No one had a fancy degree, God forbid an MBA, or had followed some cookie-cutter career trajectory. And miraculously, they had *way more money* than my friends in New York.

They drove better cars. Took better vacations. They treated themselves with more respect, from the way they decorated their homes to how they celebrated one another's accomplishments. It seemed on all counts that they lived fuller lives.

How could this be?

Well, here is where I found the keystone to this *Field Guide*: They had tried lots of different things that they already enjoyed and didn't quit until something worked. And when it worked, they went all in. That's when they won big.

Most importantly, they were comfortable with *uncertainty*.

My new friends in Miami built something they owned out of nothing.

In New York, I was handed something prefabricated. In Miami, I had no choice but to blaze my own trail.

Now before you start thinking about moving to Miami, this has nothing to do with Miami either, of course. It's your general environment and how you respond to it.

If you want to do something new and unusual, it will help to be surrounded by others who are crazy enough to be on the same mission.

Look down at your tattoo.

By embracing the unknown world of building something:
- → I abandoned titles and status
- → I delivered the maximum required
- → I risked going to zero but had unbounded upside
- → I didn't know but strived to find an answer

Futurecasting

Futurecasting is the act of creating a vivid description of where you'd like to head without having the faintest idea of how you'll get there. The "how" isn't important right now.

With a preliminary idea of who you are, from your childhood exploration or other exercises from the previous section, you're ready to create your ideal destination. For nothing will motivate you more out of this dark corner of the woods than a tasty fruit garden on the other side.

Futurecasting can be accomplished in two ways:
- → With closed eyes in a relaxed, meditative state
- → With pen and paper

The idea here is to pick a single moment and build it in your mind's eye (or on paper) as richly as possible.
- → What is your dream moment?
- → How do you feel in the moment?
- → How do others regard you?
- → How do you look?

It's helpful to return to this vision over time so it increases in resolution and emotional intensity. Don't be afraid to mold and refine this vision as you try new things and previous desires are experienced as disappointing.

By the high-fidelity nature of your futurecast, you'll know which paths could *potentially* get you there and which won't.

In other words, if you love taking a daily swim, ensure that you're positioning yourself close to the sea or a swimming pool rather than as a flight attendant.

Futurecasting will provide more information to your journey than anything you could see in the present physical world of tangled branches in front of you.

Embrace the Now

When we begin shaping where we want to go, with all the signs and sounds that accompany your desired destination, the unrefined present has the potential to look even more ugly and frightening. The woods are terrifying enough—we don't need to go about making them darker and more foreboding.

Let us pretend that our futurecast involves a vast sum of money. Should we resign ourselves to being unhappy until we attain it?

In order for us to not sign a contract for misery, we must take inventory of the things we can enjoy *right now*, the things you can treat yourself to at the present moment. Even a simple walk away from your desk for a coffee is a renowned luxury, both to the new hire and billionaire corporate raider alike.

Your inventory may look like the example below from a futurecast involving a larger amount of money.

Present inventory to enjoy:

→ Walking in the outdoors
→ Making homemade cookies
→ Talking with a friend

Future inventory to enjoy:

→ Traveling to a luxurious beach destination
→ Wearing a fine suit or couture dress to a red carpet event
→ Buying a family member a new, more comfortable home

Finally, with an inventory of what to enjoy now, we must ensure that we actually enjoy it! Don't skip the long phone calls with a friend or perfecting your chocolate chip cookie. These available rewards provide precious fuel for us to continue on our uncommon journey with an optimistic outlook.

Section 3:

MAKING YOUR FIRST STEP

There's a reason you got a tattoo on the way into the woods.

A tattoo serves to remind us of the things we don't want to forget, even when things get tough. Even when it looks like there's no one around to help us, we can help *ourselves* with a little bit of wisdom to supplement our instinct.

It's the sticky note on the side of your computer monitor or the school motto stenciled on the wall in the locker room that you tap before walking out on the field for the big game.

We can all use a reminder of the power that's already within us to survive in the woods. There's nothing in the discussion below that you'll be unable to perform, at any stage of your life.

The Power of Iteration

Iteration is the only technique that, with ample time, will get you out of *any* situation. Even with limited time, it's often the only thing we've got. Learn to get comfortable with it.

Iteration means simply trying lots of different things and slowly narrowing down the options to a solution.

The steps could be seen as:
- → Catalog various options to try
- → Group them into similar categories
- → Test the first option

And it's not always about survival. Sometimes, it's merely escaping mediocrity, the humdrum that has started to wear you down slowly.

There's always a way out of the woods. In fact, there are many ways out! You just need to begin working through potential solutions.

Like a janitor with an enormous key ring, you'll find the key that fits the lock even in the midst of hundreds of identical-looking keys. Similarly, trying the wrong key in the lock isn't a "failure," it's an iteration—just try another key.

> **Guidepost:** *Calmly trying new solutions will take you to wherever you want in life.*

The pass or fail mentality of our current school systems raises the stakes unnecessarily high for producing the wrong answer. Nowhere but in an American high school does getting the answer wrong cause so much pain and yield so little understanding. The frustration with getting things wrong is a cause for students to throw down their pencils and quit. Perhaps those same students see through the absurdity of the game altogether.

If you never stop looking for solutions, you'll find one eventually or quite literally die trying without ever tasting failure.

With iteration, there can be no failure.

Running Micro-Tests

Iteration, when recorded and organized, is the underlying skill of a Micro-Test.

A Micro-Test, or developing an MVP (minimum viable product), is the smallest particle of your Big Idea, and if it works, that suggests the whole big thing might work too.

The exercise of breaking big things into smaller pieces should become so second nature that you think of the "tests" at the same time as the big picture. You'll find that no idea is too big or too terrifying with this technique.

If your dream is to open a school for young musicians, don't go immediately renting a $10,000 per month auditorium. Rather, toss some fluorescent flyers into the hallway of the nearest high school and see if anyone emails you to sign up.

A Micro-Test is both:
→ Rapid
→ Cheap

Notice how flyers, rather than beautiful full-color pamphlets, were tossed into the hallway. This is something that everyone can afford.

> **Guidepost:** *When you're stuck with a Big Idea, direct your attention to how you could test its viability immediately.*

Many don't break ground on a grand idea because it's not easy or comfortable to shift from looking at the mountaintop to the first step. Hitting your Big Idea may require new relationships, know-how, or resources that you don't have at this present moment. That doesn't mean you can't begin to make headway with virtually *nothing*.

Even the most capital-intensive, high-risk businesses on the planet, like rocket development and space exploration, are solely funded on well-developed *ideas*. It's actually so expensive to even build a rocket prototype that often only mental hours are expended in advance.

In fact, SpaceX was founded on an idea without proof of concept. Elon Musk presented his vision to a group of aerospace engineers and investors, many of whom were initially skeptical. But Musk was persistent and convinced them to buy in.

In 2006, SpaceX launched its first rocket, the Falcon 1, which promptly crashed into the ocean. It took another two years to get it right. Since then, the company has continued to innovate and develop new technologies, such as the Falcon Heavy and the reusable Falcon 9 rocket. Today, SpaceX is one of the most successful and innovative space companies in the world.

Musk once said, "We're famous for converting things from impossible to *late*."

Here are a few common Micro-Testing strategies:
→ Simple website or lead page
→ Verbal or digital survey of strangers
→ Low-budget search ads (Google Ads or other)
→ Using a consortium of similar-minded people or an online community

This list is not exhaustive or prescriptive. Collect information in the way most accessible and relevant to you.

Learning and Review

When something doesn't work and, more importantly, when something *does* work, the result needs to be disassembled and reviewed. Otherwise, you've risked learning nothing at all, and you've surrendered the ability to replicate it.

In other words, for iteration to be a useful strategy, you can't try the key that didn't fit twice!

Some prefer checklists, spreadsheets, or notebooks

to review their week's progress. This is a sound tactic, employed by wise people all the way back to the Roman Stoic (and emperor) Marcus Aurelius.

> **Guidepost:** *Learning sounds hard. It's not. It's being sure you're not making the same mistakes (by reusing the same iterations) over and over.*

At the end of each cycle, whether it's a week or trial run, ask yourself:
→ What worked?
→ What could I do better next time?
→ What did I do that wasted time or other resources?

I track my learnings in a spreadsheet in weekly cycles. Remember, even finding that something didn't work is still progress.

Making mistakes is encouraged, but not learning from them burns time and resources.

Section 4:

ENCOUNTERING OTHER EXPLORERS

In the woods, you may find yourself crossing paths with another explorer.

After all, this is a common place to explore—it's expansive but not a vacuum. Like all encounters, some may be beneficial and some may be perilous, no matter how wide the smile of the passerby.

I've met many wonderful people and equally as many who appear wonderful but turn out to be destructive much further down the road.

If you question the passerby, you'll have a better sense of their intentions.

And don't forget to take your time. The longer you have contact with a stranger, the clearer their intentions become. Then you can determine if they align with yours.

> **Guidepost:** *Take your time when meeting other explorers, as they will reveal themselves slowly.*

The Guardian of the Status Quo

No one memorizes business failure statistics, relishes in others' misery, and is quicker to say "I told you so" than the Guardian of the Status Quo.

Sadly, this character will often take the shape of your closest friends and family. They're quick to judge and suggest the well-worn route, despite having achieved little themselves. Of course, they've risked too little and have escaped the heat of the spotlight that shines on those who are out to make big things happen.

No character appears more logical, respectable, and reasonable. "Just look at the statistics!" they might say. Listen for a chuckle when you lay out your big dream. The Guardian of the Status Quo would never consider taking such a big step—they can barely comprehend it—so can you blame them for laughing?

Helpful question: What have you done similarly to suggest you know the way better than me?

The False Guide

We all know this person: The False Guide talks in exacts and absolutes as if he has explored every inch of the woods himself. He knows where the best shelter is; he's aware of the secret path to the clearest water and finest delicacies. Perhaps he posts photos of himself online showing his carefree ways with money in a luxurious setting.

The False Guide points you in various directions and offers a wide variety of options—for a fee. He's the self-described specialist, the decorated expert, the man you're *so lucky* to meet. But there's no one you should question more than those who hand you a direct answer to your problem.

The False Guide enforces his map on you. In fact, he claims this is the only way!

Perhaps the False Guide has some value to society—he gets people up and moving. But only from a place of fear. *Look at that guy! I'd better get to work*, you think.

There's no character more misleading along your journey than the False Guide.

Helpful question: Are you sure you know where you're going?

The Thief

Upon first glance, the Thief appears to be harmless. He presents no outward threat and seems in no rush. He likes to keep things open-ended. He's a cool cat nursing a drink at the end of a long bar. A business deal may seem too good to be true. "You can pay me back later," he might say. But he's buying time, exploiting your knowledge, and gaining advantage every moment you spend with him.

The Thief believes that the only way to get ahead, to

enrich himself and survive, is to take from another. In fact, he thinks it's his duty to steal from the naive and unsuspecting. The Thief plays a highly intelligent but dangerous game.

The Thief can be tamed with legal contracts, face-to-face dealings, and leverage. Once identified, they're nothing to be afraid of: Their power is drastically overrated.

Undetected they can ruin you.

Helpful question: What exactly do you hope to gain from this interaction?

The Elder

The Elder has been through the woods so much that he's starting to look like a tree. He's taken the necessary time to understand the meanings and lessons from his journey, and his demeanor is characterized by quiet confidence, a peace of mind. He's often mistaken for the Humble Traveler in his simple mode of speech and dress.

The Elder has no need to impress. There's no lavish car, no diamond bezel on his watch, no ostentatious flourish to his step. Rather, when asked a question, the Elder will often respond with another even more pointed question that prompts you to find the answer yourself. One minute with an Elder is worth thousands of hours to a Humble

Traveler. Prepare yourself by knowing what to ask, should you be lucky enough to meet one.

You may only meet two or three Elders during the course of your entire life.

Helpful question: What are your principles to live by?

The Humble Traveler

The Humble Traveler is just like you.

He knows he doesn't know much, and he's quick to admit it. He's got a few pennies in one pocket and a dream in the other. He's working through his own journey to get to his own destination.

It's easy to befriend the Humble Traveler—there's plenty to talk about. If your interests are mutual, driving toward the same vision, you might even consider banding together after careful alignment.

Unlike many others you'll meet, the Humble Traveler will never enforce his map on you. He's often the one that believes in your own journey, while others, like the Guardian of the Status Quo, will laugh behind your back.

Helpful question: Where are you trying to get to and how can I help?

Section 5:

GENERAL HAZARDS AND ANTIDOTES

There are common hazards that will arise on a journey through the woods—both on my map and on yours.

This form of "preparation" differs from the memorization before a test or rehearsal before a speech, as the hazards I'm referring to are meaningful to remember at all times, rather than knowledge you'll soon forget after a single performance.

Comparatively, it's far better to be interested than prepared. And when you're interested, you're *always preparing*! For example, when I'm on a podcast about topics like AI or startups, it's hard to get me to *stop talking*, let alone run out of ideas to share.

> **Guidepost:** *Preparation is a survival technique for the unenthusiastic. It is no match for genuine interest.*

Nevertheless, there are some hazards you can become ready for—specifically, popular investment schemes like day trading or house flipping investments that make getting rich look straightforward. And if you think investing is "buy low, sell high," you need to read this section again.

Further, thinking you know too much is a burden far too heavy to carry. Finally, thinking you can work yourself into riches is akin to carrying stacks of lead bars.

Uninformed Investing

I've spent many years as a fixed income trader at a major investment bank and as an accredited investor moving securities around trying to make money. To the young and inexperienced me, this was a fast track to wealth and all the good things that came along with it.

From my position on a trading floor, the more strategies I learned, the more confused I got. What worked for John in crude oil never seemed to work for Doug in foreign exchange. How could it be possible that someone's map couldn't be used across similar commodities?

Even from my perspective years later as a director at a large Wall Street investment bank, I learned that most people speculating couldn't accurately explain to a third party what they were doing. I now estimate that they each built their own map and guideposts that worked *only* for them—word-of-mouth information, technology, or other proprietary models.

> **Guidepost:** *You can't learn from someone else how to trade or invest. You can only learn from doing.*

Shockingly, the maps they built weren't portable. Meaning, outside of working at a bank or hedge fund, their skills were utterly useless. They'd need hundreds of millions of dollars of cash in a portfolio to do what they did on a daily basis at their seat at a bank.

Nothing can lead would-be entrepreneurs astray like the allure of a fast buck from investing. This is a fiction portrayed in Hollywood and on social media.

Unless financial markets are your sole passion, unemotionally consider the markets and those that operate them as services and service providers. The markets have sucked in far too many unsuspecting young and talented entrepreneurs than I believe is productive.

Beware the Hazard: What's been sold to us as "investing" by social media, TV, Hollywood, and all the usual suspects isn't actually investing at all. It's blind gambling with your hard-earned money. Because if you don't have an edge, you're gambling. And you'll likely never have an edge.

Anytime you pick a stock, decide that the euro is going to fall in value versus the dollar, or buy into a new crypto project, you're gambling. In fact, whether you're investing in "highly vetted" startups or the biggest blue-chip companies in the world, you're gambling.

No matter how many computer screens you have in your home office, you don't know what the hell is going to happen to the price.

You don't have an edge. Ever. And if you do, at least in the world of public equities, you'll end up in prison if you use that edge to make money.

But you might ask, what about long-term investing? Where's Warren Buffett when you need him? I'm talking about lashing yourself to the tendency for things to grow (specifically, here in the United States at the time of writing) and the fact that there's embedded inflation in our monetary system. Meaning, even if nothing else happens, things generally go up in dollar terms over time. How thrilling!

Long-term investing is simply participating in the phenomenon that in an innovative economy things will probably grow, and they'll keep printing more and more money over the long run. That means asset prices, specifically U.S. equities, just go up over time.

Yes, it's the only way to not totally screw yourself when you're playing the markets, because you have the edge of "things going up over the long run" at your back. And indeed, if you put a small pile of money in the S&P 500 each month, when it comes to retiring thirty to forty years later there's a good chance that you'll have a bigger pile of money. But is that going to be enough for you?

Of course, you need money to invest in the first place, which you don't have when you enter the woods. So if you're earning a humble living and setting aside a few hundred dollars each month, you'll never hit the megabucks investor lifestyle being sold to you from the media.

Embrace the Antidote: *Invest in yourself* is an old, tired phrase that should be dusted off and set at the top of your to-do list. It's the most important thing you can do. Here's why:

When you invest in a stock, you have no idea what's going to happen. The price will oscillate without your control. The CEO may get caught snorting prescription drugs in the bathroom. The underlying product may end up causing skin disease and trigger billions of dollars in class action litigation. It's unlikely that you're the corporate raider who can buy up a big enough percentage of the company and start cutting the fat yourself. If you are, however, you're more than welcome to skip to the next section.

Instead, when you invest in yourself, you can make a pretty good guess at what's going to happen instead of handing over your money to a company you know little about.

When you take a painting class, you'll invariably be better at painting after the program. At the very least, you won't get *worse* at painting. This is relatively predictable.

When you read a book (like this *Field Guide*), there's a high probability that you'll learn *something*.

Even treating yourself to a gym membership or nutritious foods will have a measurable impact over time.

> **Guidepost:** *If you control the outcome from your money, you're investing. If you don't, you're gambling.*

Further, for the average investor, when a stock goes down and you lose, you've learned nothing. You just have less money now, and you're angry. You won't learn from this experience either, and most likely you'll get back to this way of "investing" (losing money) in no time.

Put that money to work by investing in you.

Thinking You Know

I visited the Liberty Science Center in Jersey City, New Jersey, when I was about ten years old. The center featured various interactive exhibits designed to get kids excited about STEM fields. Elementary and middle school students, including fully uniformed Boy Scouts, lined up to play with electricity, insects, and chemicals all from behind a safety glass, narrated by a friendly cartoon character on an old television screen overhead. The floors were striped with sneaker scuffs from the thousands of kids filtering through the museum each day.

The highlight of the trip was a pitch-black "touch tunnel" designed to simulate the experience of blindness. This experience, while frightening at first, was low risk. The tunnel was lined with soft, padded carpeting, so even if I were to stand up abruptly and hit my head, the mishap would be painless. Kids crawling behind me in the tunnel presented a feeling of urgency.

Mostly the tunnel allowed me to reach out and approximate the dimensions and path of the space without the aid of my vision. Each touch was a "bet" and a low-risk one, as touching the wall was neither painful nor costly.

A bet involves risk (touching the side of the tunnel), a thesis (what you think will happen), and an outcome (what happens).

When I made contact with the wall, I discovered "the truth." The wall is *here*. Before making these small gambles, I had no idea how the tunnel bent around me.

If the tunnel walls were electrified, however, each touch would be far riskier, and I'd make fewer moves.

When you know very little and need to make a move, the best we can do is make frequent, painless (read: low-risk) guesses.

> **Guidepost:** *Determine the cheapest bet that helps you find out the truth and make it.*

Remember your tattoo? Frequent, painless guesses is how we'll define adaptation for the time being.

Calibrate your low-risk move and make it. Most of the time, you will have *no idea* which direction to go in advance.

Beware the Hazard: There isn't a class or book for most of the unique things we want. That's how unique they are! They're quite different from what others accomplish with entirely different skill sets and dispositions.

There isn't a class for everything. That's why we find ourselves in the woods. In the woods, we don't know much of anything. And worse, thinking you know too much will get you lost forever.

Out of desperation, we make extremely risky bets: the "put it all on black" kind, where you can go broke with limited upfront information and low probability of success.

Or perhaps we enter a cycle of "learning" where we watch videos, attend seminars or talks, all with the false idea of gaining perfect knowledge before starting. Of course, in this loop, you'll never get started.

Embrace the Antidote: Roll up your sleeve and look at your tattoo. When you don't know, you can adapt—or better yet, *iterate*. That is, you can gamble a little with a thousand-sided die.

There are a few ways to bet:
→ With time
→ With reputation

- → With financial resources such as money (don't do this until you have plenty)
- → With human capital (unlikely unless you're a dictator or king)

The key here is to use as little as possible of the above resources (time, reputation, and money) to make the roll (and get an answer).

Don't spend your life savings on crafting a unique bowling shoe that you don't already have millions in standing orders for. Instead, mock up an AI illustration of the shoe and take preorders by collecting emails on a landing page without spending a cent. Yes, this is legal.

Even my writing this book is a gamble with my time. I have an edge in that I have experience writing and have been testing my *Field Guide* for years. But there's still the risk that someone out there won't buy my argument. And that's okay because it's a tiny risk, with much more upside.

Thinking Someone Else Knows

In 2019, I dreamed of making $100,000 a month.

But it wasn't an innocent high school math class dream while doodling in my notebook, it was an all-out obsession. I wanted it so bad that I went around to everyone I could find, asking them how exactly they did it. One friend of mine—I'll call him Mack—was so generous with his time that he virtually laid out the blueprint for how he built his business, which was making well over my magic number each month.

He walked me through his agency model step-by-step and suggested what products and services could be sold for the highest margin. I didn't have the slightest interest in this line of work, but I managed to replicate the business and began selling services to new customers in a few months.

I skipped through the woods and copied his map.

Within six months and with a lean team, I was making more than $100,000 a month. But there was one significant problem—I built a business I hated. I had used someone else's map. So while I *won* (to the outside world, at least) by pulling in the big bucks I had dreamed about, I truly lost in creating something that was ultimately unmanageable for me. I shut the business down several months later and started over.

I don't blame Mack. Like a good friend, he was just trying to help. It was ultimately my fault for copying someone else's map and expecting magical results.

> **Guidepost:** *If you build with someone else's map, and it somehow works out, it's a hollow victory.*

The natural inclination when lost is to call for help. This is human, and you're not at fault for attempting it. But after a few desperate hollers in the woods, you'll find it useless, energetically draining, and even more threatening as you've called dangerous attention to yourself.

And when a savior does show up, he will have all the wrong answers for you.

Beware the Hazard: Phoning a friend, attending networking events and seminars, or reading hundreds of articles and guides is great entertainment, but this won't help you escape confusion and save your business or endeavor. It will only lure you in the wrong direction.

At best, such activities are forms of procrastination that allow you to direct attention outward rather than asking yourself the right questions: Who am I? What am I good at? What do I most enjoy?

At worst, this becomes your sole strategy for decision-making, as you surrender to the false notion that someone else always knows better than you.

If you've read every how-to-get-rich blueprint and you still aren't rich, you've proven that another's map doesn't work! Obsessing over others' blueprints may permanently stall you from getting started in the first place.

Embrace the Antidote: You already know or could make a few guesses at what to do next, without asking anyone. You've just never given much authority to your own guidance. Your unfiltered intuition is a human ability—a superpower—that you must rely on in all circumstances.

For example, you may find it entertaining and pleasant to set up a small table in a busy part of your town to survey potential customers or even sell your product directly. To others, spending a night in the county jail would be preferable.

Perhaps you know that you have a certain ability and interest but still ask another party what to do—well, they would tell you to rely on digital marketing (it worked for them), leaving you scrambling to learn a suite of technology you know nothing about. All the while, you could have collected critical market data for free by hanging out in your closest city with a clipboard and table in a weekend's time.

You already know the way. Follow it.

Hard Work Is a Lie

Let's exit the woods for a moment and enter another wild and dangerous place.

If you find yourself in the open sea without a life vest, struggling, working your body against the waves, you'll soon die. But it's not the water alone that's so deadly.

After the laborious paddling, kicking, clamoring, you'll soon become exhausted and down you'll go. Your own behavior was the culprit. Many who have experience with the sea, from sailors to lifeguards, know that *relaxing*, (as difficult as it may sound), as you enter the water, whether thrown overboard or caught in a riptide, is the only way to survive.

By conserving your energy, you buy yourself time for the unknown to work in your favor. That unknown may be a fisherman or Coast Guard vessel making their evening rounds that ultimately saves your life.

Hard work won't save you in the woods either. Buy yourself some time.

Beware the Hazard: Hard work, for the sake of hard work (or because someone told you to work hard), is a guaranteed way to fail. Let's start with a few simple examples and then apply this to entrepreneurship.

A simple illustration involves a day laborer repairing a pothole in the sun. He can struggle and struggle, filling potholes all day long, but under no circumstances will he improve his condition beyond his fixed wage for his endeavors. If you think this is a discussion about opportunity, circumstances, or education, –think again.

An emergency room doctor, taking patient after patient,

will still earn a fixed salary (albeit higher than the day laborer). Still, this emergency room doc, should he fancy a villa in Lake Como and a handcrafted Hinckley boat for five-million each, will likely never be able to afford both, no matter how hard he works.

Now, an entrepreneur can toil over the *wrong problems* and build the *wrong solutions* for years! This is why I don't shudder when I hear how many businesses fail in the United States every year. Most of the business owners are simply working themselves to death on the wrong problems. Of course they went out of business!
Do you feel bad for them? Do you blame the challenges of *business itself* for their failures?

Embrace the Antidote: Take time (or buy yourself time) to consider your desires and the various ways to get there. Don't start the work, but, like a child, begin playfully planning and mentally experimenting.

In a state of calm, your perspective widens and options multiply. In contrast, when under stress, tunnel vision develops and the way out shrinks to only a few (many times wrong) options.

Even when confronting a dead-end, calm is a better way to open up your creativity to new, previously unseen options.

Sometimes a simple walk around the block after you've hit a dead end is all you need to find your next move.

The Startup Martyr

We've all heard the stories about ramen noodle diets and sleeping in cars and on beanbag chairs under a cinder block desk. Perhaps things start with meager resources. Or perhaps at some point, times do get difficult enough to merit desperate circumstances—after all, I was once so broke I had to resort to selling shoes in a men's store for near minimum wage.

In such times, of course, we have no choice but to fight our way out. But—and this is a huge but—long periods of suffering combined with hard work have the effect of weakening the explorer rather than making him stronger and more capable.

You can grind yourself to death.

> **Guidepost:** *There's a difference between struggling (healthy) and suffering (unhealthy).*

This is simply due to the fact that basic needs should be met to focus on higher order, more creative tasks.

Beware the Hazard: There's a romantic allure to suffering. It's culturally celebrated as if it's necessary to achieve any form of material success. In film and popular success stories, there's the "poverty period" that's often more romanticized than the "success period." There's no doubt that the hardship of starting with little resources builds character, but over time it can also destroy the spirit.

That's because hardship will misdirect your attention and energy. If you're sleeping poorly, your focus and creativity will be stunted. If you're eating like crap, don't expect to pull marathon workdays without crashing.

Finally, if you're constantly in a state of hardship, you haven't built a business in the first place.

Embrace the Antidote: Determine nonnegotiable aspects to your quality of life. For me, it's a gym nearby, a safe community, and a clean and quiet place to sleep. I had to leave New York for more affordable cities outside of my own country, like Mexico City, to establish this when I had little money left over to spend on my lifestyle.

In the meantime, I performed odd jobs to bring in money to fund my plans and necessities.

If you find yourself negotiating away your basic quality of life for your dream, you're diminishing yourself to a mental disadvantage.

Again, your template for baseline quality of life is yours alone to define. Do not look outside to find the answer. Layering on another template or belief system will lead to confusion and wasted time.

Take care of yourself as soon as you can afford it. This

will allow you to move faster through the woods, well rested and alert to the upcoming challenges that will surely arise.

If you're enjoying *The Entrepreneur's Field Guide*, so far, please consider leaving a review at:

www.amazon.com

This helps spread the word of entrepreneurship with more Humble Travelers like yourself.

...

80

Section 6:

BREAKING GROUND

From a Seed: Building Something New

Your business evolution truly begins when you take your insights and experiences into consideration.

Listen to who you are—dismiss the expectations branded onto you by parents, teachers, supervisors, or the world at large, and tune into the voice of your true self that bubbles up from within. Find the person inside who you're certain is *really you*.

Here's the simple formula for making headway:
- → Decide on idea or area of interest
- → Develop specific skills as needed within this area of interest
- → Determine the cheapest and fastest way to test your ideas
- → Get to work iterating!

I receive thousands of messages every month from fans on social media. Most of these—probably more than ten thousand messages—are in regard to getting started.

Want to know the secret? There is no special way to get started. You just have to make an easy, cheap first move.

> **Guidepost:** *You already own a million-dollar insight that nobody else has or can execute right this very moment.*

The easy, cheap first move need not be more than a seed, a granular element of whatever the big thing is. If the little move goes right, you can feel more confident progressing to the big thing.

In the startup world, this is called building an MVP, or minimum viable product. This is the smallest increment of your big thing that customers can play with and provide feedback.

And there are several paths through this particular neck of the woods.

From Propagation:
Buying Something Cheaply

With the advent of micro-companies, such as small software as a service (SaaS) tools developed by single engineers or small teams, the age of micro-acquisition has emerged. I'm referring to the act of buying a (very) small business, many times without existing customers.

The world of brick-and-mortar is typically too costly for new entrepreneurs. Purchasing equipment, signage, and taking on a commercial lease is generally a nonstarter—let alone taking on debt to finance something that you're unsure will succeed under your leadership.

But with digital products, the sale price can be in the low thousands. Here you can acquire the foundation of something that you can market uniquely or modify inexpensively to unlock hidden value that the seller of the company either didn't see or hadn't the patience to realize fully.

Here are the two main categories of small digital acquisition strategies:
→ Buy software and improve it
→ Buy software and market to another audience (reposition it)

If you can buy something similar to your idea and modify it, you should take the opportunity to skip far ahead by saving yourself months of development time.

> **Guidepost:** *If you're really in a rush and can afford it, buy something to breeze past hundreds of initial common mistakes.*

While you think you're paying for software, you're actually paying for:
→ The completed troubleshooting of the developer
→ The result of hundreds of iterations
→ The initial research and testing
→ The knowledge that something about this exact product still isn't quite right (otherwise it wouldn't be for sale)

And you'll get an incredible deal. Most micro-businesses are sold at a loss when the software developer's hours are taken into consideration.

Grafting: Combining Experience

If you were to meet a fellow Humble Traveler on your journey, someone who saw the woods in a complementary way, would you let this individual join your journey for a few paces?

Wilson Ruotolo, a Forbes 30 Under 30 designee, is a cofounder of Hedgehog, a robotic food production company that serves as a pristine example of combining seemingly disparate skill sets to create a powerhouse business. Wilson earned a Ph.D. in robotics at Stanford University by developing a "gentle" robotic hand that could manipulate delicate objects like fruits and vegetables.

He struggled to put his robotics to work until he met Jamie Balsillie—another Stanford grad, but from the business school—who convinced Wilson that notoriously delicate mushrooms were the biggest opportunity.

By combining robotics and agricultural know-how, Wilson and Jamie have scaled the previously unscalable—indoor mushroom cultivation, now a several billion-dollar market. This is real-life grafting.

Together, two unique parts combine to make a much stronger whole. An ideal collaborator:
- → Has a similar communication style to yours
- → Has a different skill set and lived experience
- → Is aligned both on vision and financially with the outcome of the project

As tight of a bond as was formed between Wilson and Jamie, a collaborator must be reevaluated as time goes on—there's no "set it and forget it." We're human, and our motivations and drive can ebb and flow. Realistically, the best way to maintain a relationship between you and a cofounder or collaborator is to foster an honest and open line of communication. If there's an awkward subject to breach, get it out of the way as soon as possible.

> **Guidepost:** *Look around. Do you have a perfect collaborator right in front of you?*

Finally, there must be a contractual (legal) element to any collaboration or cofounder situation. Yes, your business may not work out, certainly not the billion-dollar valuation you're hoping for, but that doesn't mean you should put ownership percentages and intended compensation aside. Think ahead—there's stress among collaborators both when things fail and when things *work*, especially for when they work out!

Your agreement should outline:
- → Who owns what
- → Who gets paid or receives a salary (if anyone)
- → How long you both intend to dedicate to the project
- → If you're able to engage in business activities outside of this project

Keep this agreement fresh and update it as necessary.

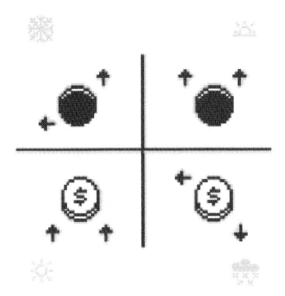

Section 7:

THE SEASONS

Each stage in your unknowing journey has a distinct season, which I'll relate to the seasons we're all familiar with in the wild.

As you move through the seasons, you can calmly and unfailingly assume that you'll make progress as long as you don't stop.

The most challenging journeys—the one you've chosen—must begin in winter.

Winter: The Season of Confusion

Capital: None
Direction: None

When you first enter the woods, very little looks familiar.

Perhaps you've just left a full-time job, or you've just graduated from college. You don't even know what you want, let alone how to get anywhere in particular.

In this season of confusion, the most important thing is to take the time to determine where you should go and then consider heading in that direction by revisiting concepts from Section 2: Taking Inventory. The more that you know yourself, the clearer the next step will become.

Here, we must play games, such as:
→ Imagine if I did this thing where I'd be in ten years

→ What is an end state I can work backward from?
→ What is a situation I'd like to avoid altogether?
→ What have I been doing that hasn't been working?
→ Are there any habits that, if removed from my life, would lead to more success with less effort?

The answers to these questions are critical. Even if you feel foolish during the exercise, I urge you to keep asking them until you come up with concrete answers. Anyone experiencing a "midlife crisis" isn't insane—they simply never bothered to take the time to address these questions and ambitions earlier in life, when they were far less disruptive to address.

During this season, expect to earn very little, so you must also buy yourself some time to think, whether it's with odd jobs, freelancing, or cutting costs. The good news is that most problems can be solved in as little as a day and very few take more than a week of attention.

You don't need to buy a one-way ticket to an Indian ashram to "find yourself" or purchase expensive and trendy guided retreats.

> **Guidepost:** *Self-discovery can never be found "out there" in a retreat, program, or travel itinerary.*

Having traveled the world myself for several years and talked with countless like-minded travelers, I know firsthand that extensive travel can be used as a form of procrastination and escaping the difficulty of looking inward. Further, as someone seeking, you don't want to surround yourself with others just as confused as you are!

As painful as it will be, sit alone with your thoughts until answers present themselves. There, of course, is no cost associated with this kind of self-reflection.

During this time of thinking and experimentation, there are a few ways to maintain a comfortable lifestyle and lower your expenses to extend your runway to think. I highly recommend taking one of these avenues.

How to survive winter:
- → Find odd jobs, gigs, and short-term projects that allow you to cover the basics but not work you to the brink of being unable to think, rest, and plan
- → Reduce unnecessary spending on things that don't bring you happiness
- → Relocate somewhere with a lower cost, yet high standard of living - this may be another city or state or another country altogether (but think Topeka, not Thailand)
- → Join together with others weathering the storm in shared housing with communal resources - "growth houses" as they're known in the startup community

How **not** to survive winter:
- → Cutting expenses to the point of physical or

mental suffering, malnutrition, or putting yourself in danger
→ Running up large credit card debt that "you'll pay back when your business works out"
→ Taking loans from family and friends
→ Traveling to "find yourself"

Remember, winter always turns to spring.

Spring: The Season of Iteration

Capital: None
Direction: Defined

The season of iteration begins once you've determined your general direction and interests.

To illustrate this section, I've purposely chosen a colorful example to highlight how unique your path may look and still "work out." I've personally seen even more unusual combinations of interests generate enormous amounts of money and happiness for others.

Let's assume that you've come to the conclusion that "I want to put my obsession with tie-dyed clothing and baseball to use." Strange? Even better.

It's time to begin iterating. Notice how specific we are with our direction. The more specific and unique your direction is, the more success you will have as you become the only person who can supply this thing to society.

Don't worry if you're not already in a creative career or haven't received a degree in art. You can start from anywhere. Everyone is equal in the woods.

Here, from our example, we can safely assume three paths to test for thirty days each:
- → Post on social media about your early shirt designs (the technique, your inspiration, your love of the process) once a day, relying on baseball metaphors as you talk
- → Make a list and reach out to other T-shirt designers who have worked with sports themes and offer to help them free of charge
- → Take old baseball jerseys and tie-dye them; tag existing and past players on the team; offer to mail them out for free

These three paths produce the similar endgame of a life filled with tie-dye and baseball. The total cost for each of these avenues should be less than one hundred dollars. You should give each path an appropriate fixed amount of time to test. Set a deadline.

You're testing for:
- → Do I actually like doing this thing?
- → Do other people enjoy when I do this thing?
- → Can I do this thing for a long period of time?
- → Did anyone already offer me money to do this thing?

If you've progressed through your three iterations and found something that creates interest, you know you've stumbled upon something valuable. If not, simply create another three tests to run.

With this framework, you will spend no more than a year picking your direction by working in three-month blocks. When most spend a lifetime unhappy with their career and lifestyle choices, a year is a small amount of time to put at risk for the potential of unlimited upside in the form of happiness, wealth, and quality of life.

Summer: The Season of Choice

Capital: Moderate
Direction: Defined

Getting results with your idea is like seeing a landmark that you recognize in the distance—you suddenly realize that you may be headed in the right direction.

Once you've received some initial feedback (sales, video views, celebrity endorsements), it's time to put the pressure on and *do more of what's working.*

From our tie-dye example above, let's assume that your Boston Red Sox jersey was reshared online and reached thousands of fans. In fact, about fifty people sent you a

DM requesting a jersey for themselves, and they're willing to open their wallets.

Here, it's safe to assume that you've created value from your interest. Commit to this direction and choose your path!

What happens next?

Double the focus on this iteration and see what happens.

In this example, you may decide to:
→ Take higher quality images of your products
→ Create a simple pricing link to take payment
→ Open an online store

This achieves two things:
→ You learn faster because you create more repetitions
→ You create more value

If you continue to see growth and excitement from people (your audience), you can buckle down and stay on this path.

You'll likely begin to see wealth appear in the form of new orders, requests for custom jerseys, and happy fans reposting your artwork.

This is where you feel as though you're wielding sheer *magic*: doing what you love and getting paid for it.

Fall: The Season of Risk

Capital: High
Direction: Well-defined

You've been well on your way growing your customer base on social media. Now, you've sold almost two hundred shirts to fans all over the world, including niche communities of baseball lovers in Europe and Asia. Things are going well, so you treat yourself to renting a nicer apartment in a quieter part of town for more restful nights of sleep after long days working on designs.

But perhaps there are other ways to combine tie-dye and baseball that you haven't explored yet? Perhaps you didn't have the resources needed to expand with the right camera, equipment, or relationships to go *really* big.

Just as a hermit crab must risk their lives to grow, crawling from one shell to another, so must you to continue your journey. That means cyclically heading back into the woods another time.

Of course, the journey back into the woods means that you're ready to bravely expand your horizons and learn more. You know that the greatest artists, with the longest careers, continued to adapt and challenge themselves to the times.

Simply put, you can't stop now!

If you were to stop, a few things would happen:
- → You'd stop having fun as you become less and less challenged
- → You don't explore your own potential, which is far greater than you realize
- → You become less valuable and put yourself at risk

Staying fresh and challenged is a requirement. So having saved up about five thousand dollars from jersey sales, you decide to create another product line, a tie-dyed baseball in team colors.

Expanding from your new comfort zone looks like:
- → Trying new product lines
- → Delivering to new markets
- → Increasing production to meet demand and reduce a waiting list

Like everything else, you start small to test it, with a few baseballs of the most popular teams, with die-hard fans. A few orders come in. Then a few more. Now, the combined sales of your jerseys (which you've raised in price) and baseballs are earning you twice as much as you made in your previous job.

You soon realize that even from a place of knowing, you need to frequently step out into the unknown, into the woods.

From your place in fall, you will soon find yourself back in winter as you experiment and grow, returning to a state of unknowing. Perhaps you decide to sell your beloved business altogether to investors and start over from scratch on a new idea.

You now see how cyclical the seasons are and anticipate them with intrigue, not fear.

Systems That Replace You

One day, you'll get too big. Your rucksack will be filled with gold coins. Your success will become a dangerous weight that threatens to stop you in your tracks.

What do you do?

Whether it's producing art, software development, or home building, as your success mounts you can first turn to technology and automation to augment your processes. Then adding capable people to your team is the next step.

To replace "you" is to build systems and people around you who can deliver the quality service that you offered previously to customers yourself. The trick here is to increase output without losing the caliber of output. You don't need to compromise on the amazing experience you delivered yourself.

Standard operating procedures (SOPs) are a series of exact steps that a member of your team must follow precisely. Here, you can formalize everything from customer response emails to how to deal with each and every situation that arises in your business. In a sense, it's automation for people to ensure they deliver the best possible customer experience.

And here is where you can share the wealth that you've built with others, which helps them learn and grow.

How does this look in practice?

Certainly you may encounter far more dangerous bears in the woods, so it may be useful to share an example from a company that produces the cuddly, plush variety.

Build-A-Bear Workshop is known for its consistent and memorable in-store experience that wows customers every time they visit. The company achieves this by implementing specific standard operating procedures that help to maintain a high level of customer experience. While it seems as though each team member is being spontaneous and fun with their product walk-through, it's actually an identical script that they use from customer to customer, optimized for the Build-A-Bear experience.

Some SOPs include:
1. Comprehensive training program: All employees undergo a comprehensive training program that covers the company's core values, customer service procedures, and product knowledge. This training is standardized across all locations to ensure consistency.

2. Shadowing experienced staff: New employees are paired with experienced staff members to observe and learn from their work. This helps to make certain that all employees have a thorough understanding of the company's procedures and best practices.
3. Knowledge testing: Employees are required to pass knowledge tests to maintain a thorough understanding of the company's products and procedures. This helps to ensure that all employees have the same level of knowledge and expertise.

SOPs are the only way of building a team around your ideas that you can afford.

With a team and carefully organized procedures, you can travel for miles without fatigue.

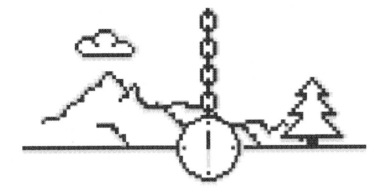

Section 8:

UNCOVERING HIDDEN TREASURE

After shutting down my digital agency in 2019 (the business I built with another's map from Section 5), and having absolutely no idea what to do next, I made a promise to myself—I was only going to do things I enjoyed and never suffer for making money again.

Because short-form content was exploding in popularity online and it was entirely free for me to try, I promised myself to post a single video a day on TikTok for thirty days. I wouldn't tell anyone about my experiment, to prevent making a show of my unlikely task of gaining internet fame.

On Day 17, after posting a variety of things I cared about—business, marketing, traveling, and fitness—I ran out of ideas and posted a skit from my kitchen table about how two different people, one "rich" and one "really rich," would interact with a server at a restaurant. Overnight, about five million people had watched the video. I had no idea what I did or how I did it.

Of course, this discovery was a result of a costless Micro-Test—this was the *only* way I could have "struck gold." Never did I ever think I could create interest on social media, let alone earn over a billion video plays.

Once things began to work, I ensured I was paying attention and learning from each iteration so that I could continue to replicate my initial accidental success.

Accidental Discoveries

X-rays: Wilhelm Conrad Röntgen's discovery of X-rays in 1895 is considered one of the most significant accidental discoveries in the field of physics. By enclosing a discharge tube in a sealed, dark carton and using a paper plate coated with barium platinocyanide, fluorescent effects were observed even when the plate was two meters away. Further experiments revealed that objects of varying thickness displayed different transparency when exposed to the rays and recorded on a photographic plate. This groundbreaking work led to the first X-ray image, capturing the shadows of bones of his wife's hand. The discovery of X-rays revolutionized medical imaging and had a profound impact on fields such as diagnostics, non-destructive testing, and scientific research. Röntgen's accidental discovery earned him the first Nobel Prize in Physics in 1901.

Post-it Notes: The invention of Post-it Notes is another famous accidental discovery. In 1968, a scientist named Spencer Silver was attempting to create a strong adhesive at 3M but ended up creating a weak adhesive instead. Years later, another 3M employee, Art Fry, found a use for the weak adhesive when he needed a bookmark that wouldn't damage his papers. This serendipitous discovery led to the creation of the widely popular and versatile Post-it Notes.

Microwave ovens: Percy Spencer, an engineer at Raytheon Corporation, accidentally discovered microwave heating in 1945. While working on a military radar project, he noticed that a chocolate bar in his pocket had melted due to the microwaves emitted by the magnetron. Spencer further experimented and developed the first microwave oven. This accidental discovery revolutionized cooking methods and paved the way for the widespread use of microwave ovens in households around the world.

Both in myth and in practice, hidden treasure is always stumbled upon. Even in pirate tales, the "treasure map" is always wrong. The X never quite marks the spot—that would be too dull!

Essentially, something as hidden (and as valuable) as treasure can only be found by trying things that previous explorers didn't attempt.

In other words, you have to try new things in the woods in order to strike gold. You may have to try things that others believed would never work themselves. There simply is no other way.

The more you avoid hazards and iterate, the more treasure you will stumble upon. Treasure appears in several ways:
- → Requests to buy something that you haven't yet offered for sale (product or service)
- → Enormous sales for new and experimental products
- → Opportunities to meet and connect with powerful people
- → Overnight fame and audience

One may be tempted to puff out their chest at the discovery of treasure and shout, "Look what I did!" You must remember that you didn't discover the treasure out of knowing, but rather of *not knowing* and iterating!

Be humble with your winnings.

It's far better to quietly unpack the treasure and determine if there are any replicable steps to how you found it. You may want to ask yourself:

→ Why am I uniquely equipped to have found this treasure?
→ Why did I find it now and not yesterday?
→ If I were to tell anyone how I found it, would they also have been able to find it too?

Once you have an idea for why things worked out, you can attempt to test it in practice to see if you can uncover more and more treasure.

Anyone who consistently succeeds, whether it's an athlete winning championship rings or an entrepreneur selling multiple startups, knows how to iterate and learn.

Section 9:

HOMECOMING

There's something that irreversibly changes in you after a long journey.

You may never be quite the same after spending time in the woods. To outsiders, after you've built something and it works out, you're unrecognizable.

There's a special confidence that's built during your time in the unknown.

Because if you're comfortable in the unknown, when are you uncomfortable? Isn't life itself a journey through the unknown?

You may find a trip to the convenience store a rare pleasure for the opportunity to "see what happens" when you're extra kind to a cashier by complimenting their customer service or buying an extra pack of gum for the kid behind you in line. You start to look at the entire world as a canvas to experiment with.

Life is the woods!

Nevertheless, like an epic saga, the hero (this includes heroines as well, but for simplicity, I'll say "hero") eventually must return home. This journey may have taken his whole life—in and out of the woods, learning and growing. At some point, he may choose to slow down.

Upon returning home, the hero shares the wisdom he learned *out there* to the kind and gentle folks who didn't have the courage to leave home. And that's okay—

it's not a hero's duty to urge people into the darkness against their will.

During his reception, the hero will speak of wonders and battles that no one could possibly understand from their vantage point. If you've never faced a dragon or one of Homer's Sirens, it will be awfully difficult to imagine confronting one.

Beyond the entertainment, the beauty of these tales, are the *underlying lessons* that shake out of the retelling of adventure. These lessons prove far more valuable than the entertainment provided by the adventure. Only you can pull the lessons from the story that's most valuable for you.

A good lesson or guidepost:

> → Is valid across history (I don't believe Homer mentioned dropshipping)
> → Is executable by you
> → Is easy to understand and share

I tell you this because someday you will be the hero I'm speaking of.

Without sharing your wisdom, a piece of your journey and sacrifice goes to waste into the molten earth to never be shared again. And this is an unforgivable crime.

Notice how many successful entrepreneurs voluntarily adopt the role of an educator and policymaker after they've earned far more than they (and their family) could spend over several generations. This is no accident.

They feel the human urge to return the wisdom back to the community at large. It's a natural inclination, and this is the only thing I will declare as mandatory from this *Field Guide*—give back generously!

But, of course, we're not there yet.

So roll up your sleeve to receive your tattoo, cast aside your desire to know, and head on off in the direction that feels most true as you descend bravely into the woods.

If you enjoyed *The Entrepreneur's Field Guide*, please consider leaving a review at:

www.amazon.com

This helps spread the word of entrepreneurship with more Humble Travelers like yourself.

•••

Bonus:

DISCOVERY WORKSHEET

What season (Confusion, Iteration, Choice, Risk) am I in right now?

_____
_____
_____

When was a time I followed another's map and didn't get the desired results?

_____
_____
_____

Who are the Guardians of the Status Quo that I need to minimize or eliminate from my journey?

_____
_____
_____

What is something I care deeply about?

_____
_____
_____

What is something I know about of which others know little?

_____
_____
_____

What are some combinations of skills that make me one of a kind?

_____
_____
_____

What would be my dream idea?

_____
_____
_____

What are three things I can test today to prove my idea?

_____
_____
_____

If my idea doesn't work at first, what are three other similar ideas I can explore?

_____
_____
_____

Is it better to start from scratch, buy another company for a head start, or collaborate with someone else to get started today?

_____
_____
_____

How will I measure my success? In money, relationships, notoriety, or other terms?

_____
_____
_____

Is there an Elder in my life I can safely share my success with?

_____
_____
_____

How can I comfort myself when things get invariably tough and confusing?

_____
_____
_____

...

Get the new digital course

The Entrepreneur's Field Guide: The Guided Journey

now at:

www.nicholascrown.com

Made in the USA
Las Vegas, NV
08 September 2023